Operation Kalulu

By the Same Author

Poetry

Napolo Poems (Manchichi)
Napolo and the Python (Heinemann)
Epic of the Forest Creatures (WASI)
Breaking the Beadstrings (WASI)
Python! Python! (WASI)
The Vipya Poem (WASI)
Ndakatulo za Napolo (Manchichi)

Plays

The Rainmaker (Popular Publications)
Wachiona Ndani? (Dzuka)
Sister! Sister! (WASI)
Achiweni Wani? [*Wachiona Ndani?* trans. by A. Mbwana] (Manchichi)

Novels

The Basket Girl (Popular Publications)
The Wrath of Napolo (WASI)
The Hyena Wears Darkness (WASI and Luviri Press)

Children's Literature

Caves of Nazimbuli (Popular Publications and Luviri Press)
Child of Clay (Popular Publications and Luviri Press)

Short Stories

Tell me a Story (Dzuka)

Folklore

Malawian Oral Literature (Center for Social Research)
Napolo ku Zomba (Manchichi)

Criticism

The Culture of Democracy [with Moira Chimombo] (WASI)

General

Directory of Malawian Writing (Dept of Arts and Crafts)
Malawian Oral Literature (Luviri Press)

Operation Kalulu

Retold by
Steve Chimombo

Luviri Press

Mzuzu
2021

First published 1994 by Popular Publications

Luviri Press
P/Bag 201 Luwinga
Mzuzu

ISBN   978-99960-66-70-2
eISBN 978-99960-66-71-9

Front cover design © Z.C. Chimombo 1994

Back cover photograph by Moira Chimombo

Printed by Lighting Source

Dedication

To Simika, who told me the fuller version of the story.

Contents

Chapter 1: The Drought   9

Chapter 2: Digging the Well   15

Chapter 3: Water is Found   21

Chapter 4: Gwape on Guard   28

Chapter 5: Fisi on Guard   35

Chapter 6: The Zombie   43

Chapter 7: Kamba on Guard   51

The End   58

Glossary   59

INTRODUCTION TO THE FIRST EDITION

The Hare and the Well is one of the commonest and most popular trickster stories in Africa. There are several versions in existence. In this retelling, I have incorporated the plots from different versions into one composite whole for dramatic effect. I hope the results are satisfactory from a modern storyteller's point of view.

As usual in my retelling of folk stories, I do not prefer one version to another. However, in my opinion, the originals are always the better versions because of the oral performance. They are also better because they keep on inspiring me in my own efforts to recapture and reconstruct them for a modern literate audience.

It is not only the oral performance that has been lost. I had to discard some accompanying songs that were almost untranslatable. I also had to underplay the fact that all the characters in this story were animals, therefore, they could not use human tools for digging a well, or even use human language. The fun, however, is to have this double knowledge and still pretend that the story is credible.

7

INTRODUCTION TO THE SECOND EDITION

Folk stories provide a wonderful way to probe the foundational beliefs of the culture of any society. Hence the need to ensure the continued availability of written versions of these stories. This particular story, The Hare and the Well, retold as *Operation Kalulu*, tells of a time of severe drought, when the animals get together to discuss what to do. Hare suggests that the animals identify a place where there was a pool before and dig there, as the water is likely to be closer to the surface. The King of the animals, Elephant, advises all the animals to come to the work place the next day, to start digging. All except Hare turn up. The pattern is repeated day after day, until the well is dug. The animals then establish rules for drawing water, one of which is that, since Hare did not help in digging the well, none of his family should be allowed to draw water. Guards are set over the well, but, one after another, they are too easily distracted away from the well by Hare's offers of food, so that Hare's family is able to draw water, until Tortoise manages to capture Hare.

This story illustrates good and bad character traits, and also the basic cultural value of community cooperation as seen in the attitudes to planning skills, work ethic, punctuality, and schedules in relation to the hard work of digging the well; health and hygiene as they relate to the excuses Hare gives for not turning up to help; and crime and punishment in connection with Hare's bribes.

CHAPTER ONE

The Drought

It was the year of the drought. Some of the oldest members pronounced it the worst drought in living memory. Others called it the grandmother of all droughts. Everything, everywhere, was dry, dry, dry. The grass had long ago wilted and lay flat, if it had not already burst open in the searing heat. The leaves had long ago dropped off from their branches and lay crackling on the ground.

The earth lay panting in the dry heat. Dust storms swirled on the dry plains. Whirlwinds raced each other across the mountain slopes. The earth shimmered and mirages danced on the horizon as if there was water just over the next rise. But there was no water anywhere. The Mtalika mountain rivers, even Mzimundilinde, had long ago dried up, mere gashes on the brows and cliffs staring up to the empty hazy skies above. Down in the valleys, the gullies told their own stories of barrenness and dryness.

It was indeed the grandmother of all droughts. It was feared that if it continued like this for another month or so the land would turn into a desert. The babies born in this year were named after it. So there was little Chilala, drought, born into this family and there was Njala, hunger, born into that family. And there was Ilikutali Mvula, the rains are far away, here, and Ndinyemeleko, give me a bit, there. Yet there was very little to eat, the granaries had been emptied months ago, they had now been upturned to show how empty they were. People trekked far and wide hunting for food in the next village. But the next village was in similar distress.

9

In Nyakalambo forest, the birds had stopped chirping to preserve the little moisture and strength left. The cicadas and the crickets had long ceased serenading each other. There was no joy in anyone's throat. No happiness in anyone's sunken eyes. Only certain knowledge that if the drought persisted there would be skeletons dropping to the ground one by one. The sounds of mourning were everywhere, greeting the forest every other day or night. Soon no one would have the strength to dig any more graves, let alone to cry at funerals or burials.

It was at the peak of this terrible drought that a meeting of all animals was called. Njobvu, the elephant, the king of all the beasts, invited all the animals to come to a meeting under the big baobab tree in the center of Nyakalambo forest. The animals, big or small, traipsed in with their families to answer the call. The lion and the leopard, the buffalo and the antelope, the rhinoceros and the duiker, the tortoise and the hare, everyone assembled at the foot of the baobab tree. There they stood, on their hooves or paws, there they squatted or sat on their haunches, as they waited for their leader to speak.

Njobvu stood facing them, his short tail against the gnarled trunk of a baobab. His grey brown skin was indistinguishable from the bark of the tree he was leaning against. He could have been just as old as the ancient tree itself. His ears flapped wide and loud for attention. His tusks reared high as if he would roar, but his voice, when it came, was low and grave.

"My brothers and sisters," Njobvu began, "I need not tell you why I have called this meeting. We all know why we are here. We are here because we are hungry and thirsty, and soon we shall perish if the drought continues. The drought cannot grow worse than this and we cannot die faster than we have been doing …. I have one question to

10

ask. It is a question which we have all been asking ourselves. It is a question we have dreaded asking each other, but we cannot continue avoiding it. We avoid it at our peril. The question is: What shall we do?"

The question reared its ugly head over them, around them, and into them. The animals quivered inwardly, they groaned and squirmed uneasily where they stood or sat. They avoided each other's eyes for fear that they would find the same dread written there.

"Yes, indeed, the chief has asked a very good question: What shall we do? It is a question pregnant with sorrow. Yet we do have to answer it soon, before we all die, one by one."

It was Kalulu, the hare, who had broken the awful silence. He was on his short stump of a tail, his forepaws waving the hot dry air in front of him. Everyone wondered why he should repeat Njobvu's question when all who had assembled there had heard it clearly; when they had been asking themselves the same question all these days, weeks, and months. But then, Kalulu was like that: He talked and loved listening to himself talking. But, when it came to action, he was the furthest away. He let others DO everything.

"By the grace of Chauta," Mkango, the lion, said, "We have survived so far. I don't believe Chauta will let us die. However, as we all know we've got to do something quickly."

Mkango's golden mane had long gone dirty brown, wilted and stuck to his skin. It no longer flowed loosely and extensively around his head. Below the emaciated head and shoulders, you could count the ribs down to his shrunken stomach. He who stood magnificently among the cats and other animals now looked as if he was on his last legs.

"It is not the problem of water alone," Chipembere, the rhino, joined in. "We don't have food to eat. We cannot bear the brunt of both hunger and thirst combined. We are surely going to die."

It was clear that anyone who spoke was going to repeat what had already been said or would state the obvious.

"Let's not confuse the issues here," Kalulu jumped in again. "Let's solve one problem at a time. If we try to combine water and food problems we will be going around in circles."

"But these are related problems," Njati, the buffalo, butted in. "You solve one, the other is also solved."

"Just like that?" Kalulu snorted. "You don't always find water with food."

"Food grows where water is."

"Let's find the water, then."

"Where?"

"You are right," Njobvu intervened. "You are both right: Where there's water there must also be food. However, first things first. Let's find the water."

"Where? We have bashed our heads over that question." Kalulu was on his feet. "I believe it is the wrong question to ask."

"Shut up, Kalulu," roared Nkhoma, the cliff hopper. "All you ever do is talk, talk, talk. I wonder how you get on with your family. You are all yappers."

"Shut up, yourself."

"Stop quarrelling, you two."

"At least give me a chance to explain why I said so."

"Go ahead."

"If we keep asking ourselves where we shall find water, we are going to do so till the last one of us drops dead on his feet. We have been asking ourselves the same question all these months and have not found the answer. We have searched for the answer in the hills and valleys, the *dambos* and plains, till we have drained the last drop where we found it. Now there's no drop left, so the question is no longer where shall we find water."

"Do come to the point."

"I WAS coming to the point," barked Kalulu. "So the practical and immediate question now is: How shall we get water?"

"How?" groaned the whole congregation.

"Yes, how?" Kalulu danced on his haunches. He knew he had them puzzled but also interested. He enjoyed the attention he was getting.

"I don't see the difference between where and how," Fisi, the hyena, spoke for all the animals.

"If we have searched high and low for water," Kalulu ignored the hyena, "and cannot find it any longer, then we have got to find a way of making the water come to us."

"We can't make it rain."

"No, but we can dig a well."

"Dig a well?"

"It is the only answer now."

"But all the wells have long since dried up, too."

"There must be a well somewhere which we can re-dig. If we dig deep enough, we are surely going to come across water."

"The little one," Mkango said thoughtfully, "seems to make sense."

"It certainly makes sense to some of us," Kalulu said proudly.

"Then," Njati said ponderously, "we come back to the same question: Where shall we dig the well?"

"That's when 'where?' comes in most usefully." Kalulu skipped up and down. "This is the low side of Nyakalambo forest stretching

13

from the slopes of Mtalika Mountain down to the valley. There must be water near the surface somewhere."

"We seem to agree, then," Njobvu came in again, "that we must think, not in terms of looking, but digging for water. Where to dig is the immediate question."

"Let's find an old well," Nkhoma opined. "A once big and flourishing well. As Kalulu here said: If we dig deep enough we surely must come across water trapped underneath."

"We all know our favorite drinking pools," Njobvu reminded all of them. "Which one seems most likely to you?"

"Njota Pool!" There was a chorus from several throats.

Njota Pool was biggest and deepest in Mzimundilinde, in the thickest part of Nyakalambo forest. In fact, it had also been the last one to dry up. All the animals had congregated closer and closer to Njota as it yielded its last drops to their parched throats. Now they had to go back to it for its deeper resources.

"All right, then," Njobvu said, "Njota Pool it shall be. We can't start on it today, as the sun is already going down. Let's sleep on it. Tomorrow at dawn, let's all meet at Njota Pool. Work starts at the crack of dawn."

The animals dispersed. Some were already beginning to feel more hopeful with the thought of digging a well. Others remained despondent: How can there be water under a dried-up pool?"

CHAPTER TWO

Digging the Well

Njota Pool stretched from here to there at its widest part. It was part of Mzimundilinde River which started from Mtalika Mountain, flowed through the pool, and went on to the muddy lake down in the plains below. The pool itself sloped gently from the top but sheered down more sharply toward the center. At its deepest part, two elephants standing one on top of the other could not be seen from the banks. Various layers of soils could be seen on the sides of the now dried-up pool as you went deeper to the bottom. That Njota Pool had dried up at all merely confirmed that this indeed was the severest drought of the century.

The animals congregated at the edge of Njota Pool at dawn, as arranged. Work did not start, however, until Njobvu took the roll call.

"Kaphulika!" trumpeted Njobvu.

"Here!" grunted the warthog.

"Mbizi!"

"Here!" answered the zebra.

"Nyamalikiti!"

"Sir!" That was the giraffe.

"Nyani!"

"Yes!" grinned the monkey.

"Mvuu!"

"Yeah!" snorted the hippo.

Njobvu went down the list: antelope, buffalo, cheetah, duiker.

"Kalulu!"

No answer.

"Kalulu!"

No answer.

"Has anyone seen the hare?"

No answer. They looked around.

"It seems," Nkhoma volunteered, "that he's not here."

"Nor his wife."

"His children?"

"None, sir."

"But he was with us yesterday."

"Yes, chattered the most and got us to come to dig the well."

"What did I tell you?" Nkhoma asked no one in particular. "I told you he is all talk, talk, talk, but when it comes to working he is miles away."

"Shut up all of you," Njobvu ordered. "We can still dig a well without him and his family. You, Nkhoma, after work, go and find out what happened to him."

"Yes, sir," answered the cliff-hopper.

Njobvu went on with the register: otter, pig, leopard, lion, till all the animals were accounted for. So it was only the hare and his family that were missing.

Work started when the sun was already high in the sky. The animals worked in family groups to ensure that everyone contributed equally. So when it was the turn for the lemurs, one family went to dig, another stayed on top to receive the soil as it was passed to them from below, and they threw it on the banks. When it was the turn of hyenas they did the same, and others cleared the banks, so that more earth could be dumped easily over the side. The well got deeper and deeper as the sun sailed higher in the sky.

The animals dug and dug; the soil was scooped out and thrown over the side. They dug and dug, and the earth was removed and thrown onto the banks. As soon as one family of animals got tired, another took its place. The relieved families rested on the banks under any shade they could find under the stripped trees that grew around the pool. The reeds and marshes had also long dried up: they now provided some protective matting on the hot ground. They had been ground to pulp by the trampling hooves and paws, so the animals did not come into direct contact with the earth.

Midday. The sun shone pitilessly overhead. Njobvu called for a break. The animals rested. Those who had a little food shared it. Grateful mouths gulped it down. Others took a nap. The talk came back to the hare family.

"He could be sick!" suggested Gwape, the deer.

"They can't all be sick," scoffed Nyalugwe, the leopard. "It's one of their tricks to shun work."

"I bet they'll drink the water together with us when we're finished."

"No way!" A chorus of protest. "How can they, when they did not help us?"

"They might come to join us tomorrow."

"We'll see."

Work resumed after a while. The sun's heat had not abated. A group of four went down the hole, the rest stood on the edge of the shaft to receive the dug-up soil. They dug and dug. They scooped and scooped, and threw the earth on the growing banks of Mzimundilinde. As soon as one group tired another group took over. The relieved family went back to rest on the banks of the river.

The afternoon wore on and the animals worked on. The dry earth churned in the pit and clouds of dust flew to the surface, choking those waiting to reach down for the dug-up earth to throw it away on top. It was worse in the hole, as the dry dust got into their mouths,

17

nostrils, ears, and eyes. The animals gagged, choked, and sneezed, but they worked on and on as they dug and dug, scraped and scooped. Njobvu stopped the work at sunset.

"It's been a hard day," Njobvu said. "It's been good work, too, but let's stop here for now. Tomorrow work starts as usual: at the crack of dawn."

*   *   *

Nkhoma, the cliff-hopper, did not forget his mission. Although worn out after the hot, hard day's labors, he took the path that led to the hare's compound. It was not difficult to find: He had been there before on different occasions. Not that he was a frequent visitor: the hares were not friends of his. In any case it was not easy to be a friend of the hares. They acted as if they were too clever for everyone else around them. They set themselves apart as if no one could excel them in anything. If the hare had been bigger, Nkhoma thought, say like the buffalo, they would have set themselves up as the leaders of all the animals. But the hares were handicapped by their size. However, they compensated for this lack of leadership qualities by taking every opportunity to trick their fellows; sometimes they even broke their own record by outwitting each other. No day passed without one outrage or another having been perpetuated. Even when the hares seemed to be doing nothing you could not be sure that they had already done it but no one had as yet realized. Nkhoma had grown up with his father's advice: Beware of those little fellows, they can out-trick even their wives, husbands, or kids. So Nkhoma always gave the hares a wide berth. He only went to see them when forced to do so, as he was doing now. He hoped he would return home unscathed.

"Ndakupha!" Nkhoma heard an ejaculation from the hare. There was the sound of a whirl, then another triumphant shout. "I've killed you!"

Nkhoma crept up to the hare's house. Kalulu was playing *nsikwa* with his family. The game consisted of two teams facing each other, a few feet apart. A row of maize cobs was in front of each team. The contest was to hit the opponent's cobs with your spinning top. If the cob fell down, you scored a point. *"Ndakupha!"* The ejaculation was to announce a score. Nkhoma stood by the doorway, fascinated by the spectacle of Kalulu, a daughter, and a son, against his wife, a son, and another daughter.

"Odi!" Nkhoma brought his presence to the notice of the contestants.

"Oh! It's you!" Kalulu jumped up. The rest, startled in their game, looked up guiltily.

"Yes! It's me!"

"Well, don't just stand there staring, sit down and join us in *nsikwa.*

"I can't sit down," Nkhoma said uneasily. "I am on an errand."

"What errand?"

"I have been sent by the chief."

"What about?"

"He wants to know why you did not come to dig the well as agreed."

"I've been sick – we've all been sick. We've just recovered."

"You can't all have been sick."

"We all were," reiterated the head of the family. "It must have been something we ate. It disagreed with us. We all had a bout of diarrhea. We couldn't have come to the well like that. Just imagine all of us disappearing into the bushes every other minute. It would have been embarrassing all around."

"Well," Nkhoma said morosely, "I'm only a messenger. I'll report what you've told me to Njobvu tomorrow."

"Do," Kalulu said carelessly, "and give him my regards."

"Aren't you coming tomorrow?"

"Of course, I am – we are, we will be there!"

Nkhoma turned away from the doorway. He retraced footsteps.

"Ndakupha!" Kalulu shouted, as Nkhoma retreated and the hares resumed their game.

CHAPTER THREE

Water is Found

At dawn the animals again assembled at Njota Pool. Before they resumed the work, Njobvu took the roll call, as before.

"Fisi!"

"Here!" the hyena answered.

"Gwape!"

"Present!" The deer was on his feet.

"Kamba!"

"Sir!" answered the tortoise.

They were called: the cat, the lizard, and the kudu.

"Kalulu!"

No answer.

"Kalulu!"

No answer.

"Has anyone seen the hare?"

No answer.

"Nkhoma!"

"Sir!"

"Did you go to the hare's house yesterday?"

"I did, sir!"

"What do you have to report?"

"I found him – I mean I found them all, playing *nsikwa.*"

"Playing *nsikwa!*" Njobvu was incredulous. "Not even playing sick?"

21

"He said they had been sick in the morning but they were recovering in the afternoon."

"What was wrong with them?"

"Diarrhea, sir. They said they could not come with it to the well, sir. So they decided to stay at home."

"But did they look sick at all?"

"They looked all right to me. As if they had not been sick at all."

"There's nothing we can do now. Let's get to work."

The animals started the work for the day. The sun was way up in the sky as the first group went down the shaft. The rest clustered round the edge to reach down for the earth that was brought up by those below. They dug and dug. They scooped and scraped.

By midday, the shaft was so deep that ten elephants standing on each other could not be seen on the banks. The steps dug in the sides of the walls of the shaft proved useless, even dangerous, to climb up and down.

"We need pulleys!" Njobvu announced. "Let's cut down some trees and get some strong bark rope together."

The best part of the afternoon was spent constructing a makeshift structure that covered the mouth of the shaft from one end to the other. A rope was tied to a crossbar that was rotated like a winch to wind and unwind a rope. The small animals and the earth containers could go up and down in this way.

"Nkhoma!" Njobvu called out at sunset, before dismissing the animals for the day.

"Yes, sir?"

"Go to the hare again. Find out what's stopped them from coming to work today."

"Yes, sir."

Nkhoma wondered why Njobvu picked on him. Any other animal could serve as a messenger. Sending him again two days running would seem as if he was spying on the hare family.

"Here comes Nkhoma!" One of the hare's sons spotted him from a distance.

"Here I am again!" Nkhoma admitted, "On the same errand."

"Our diarrhea has recurred."

"But I just saw you wrestling with your eldest son."

"It attacks us in the morning and eases up in the afternoon."

"You can't join us in the afternoon?"

"We can't trust that it is gone completely."

"Why were you wrestling then?"

"For the exercise. Diarrhea can completely drain you. So to regain strength we wrestle."

"You can regain strength digging the well."

"We just told you why we can't!"

The exasperated Nkhoma left the hares to their games and went back home. He did not believe a word he had heard from the hares.

*   *   *

It went on like that for several days. The animals dug and dug. The well got deeper and deeper. Sometimes the animals got despondent and wanted to give up. Njobvu, however, exhorted them. At other times, there was renewed enthusiasm as they felt some dampness in the soil.

"It won't be long now," Njobvu would say, inspecting the soil sample. "Look how the earth even smells of wetness."

Not many could smell the wetness. They sniffed with disbelief, but carried on doggedly with the work.

The hare and his family never put in an appearance. Njobvu even stopped Nkhoma from going to find out how the hares were faring.

"Leave them!" Njobvu ordered.

* * *

"The earth has turned moist!" someone shouted down the shaft. "Look!"

A lump of soil was relayed up and everyone crowded round to take a look.

"Yes!" pronounced Njobvu. "It's really wet."

The lump was passed round. Parts crumbled damply in the eager hands. There was jubilation all round.

"We'll find water soon."

Renewed vigor and enthusiasm went into the work the rest of the day but the consistency of the soil did not change.

"Perhaps tomorrow!" were everyone's parting words at the end of the day.

The morrow came and the labors continued with the same hare family missing.

"I see," Mkango observed, "our little friends are still sick."

"I don't believe their diarrhea story," snorted Mvuu. "The little devils ought to be strung on the nearest tree."

By mid-morning the animals were sure they would find water. The earth got damper and damper, the containers carried mud, not dry soil. Some animals actually tried to suck the water out of the mud, but only swallowed mud for their pains. Others rubbed the mud over their bodies to cool themselves.

"We will have it by evening," Njobvu reassured everyone when they resumed the work in the afternoon. But by sunset only more mud came out.

A surprise waited for them the following morning. The first group of animals that went down the shaft splashed into ankle deep water that had collected overnight.

24

"Water!" There was shouting down the shaft.

"Water!" The shout was taken up by everyone.

"We've found it!"

A bucket was sent up precipitately. Everyone was ecstatic, if not hysterical, as they scrambled to the edge of the hole. The bucket spilled as violent hands reached for it.

"Order! Order!" Njobvu shouted.

Njobvu rescued the bucket before it was smashed. He held it high in his trunk where no one could reach it.

"My dear brothers and sisters," he announced, "This is the moment we have all been waiting for. This is the reward for our hard days of labor. This is water. If it can collect like this overnight, it means there's plenty down there. Let's dig deeper, otherwise we will not have enough to go around."

More muddy water was dug and drawn up. Some animals sucked the mud for the delicious liquid. Those with parched throats waited patiently for their turn. It was soon obvious that they could not dig anymore since now there was more water than mud. The diggers were already up to their ears in waters; they would drown in it.

"That'll do for now," Njobvu ordered. "Everyone out and let's have a drink as a reward for our labors."

The diggers surfaced from below. Water was liberally shared round. The animals' relief and jubilation rang through Nyakalambo forest.

"My dear brothers and sisters," Njobvu called an impromptu meeting. "Our reward is down there. It is all there for us to drink. We can even think of starting a small garden on the banks to grow some food to stave off starvation. But before we consider those long-term projects, there is an immediate problem. You all know how we have

25

toiled daily to find this water. And you all know who has not been working with us. What do we do with the hare family?"

"They should have none of the water!" was the unanimous reply.

"But how do we stop them from getting our water?"

"Place guards round the well, day and night."

"What should the guards do to the hare if he comes!"

"Capture him and hang him on the nearest tree." Mvuu was still for strangling the hare.

"Capture him and bring him to court."

"All right then," Njobvu conceded. "Gwape!"

"Yes, sir!"

"You are going to be the first guard. Be on the lookout. Don't go to sleep, day or night. We'll send some food for you before the change of guards, in a day or two."

"Yes, sir."

Nkhoma was relieved. He had been afraid that he would be the first to be put on guard. As the animals went joyously home Nkhoma took the path to the hare family. He had to tell them the good and the bad news. He did not find it strange to be the bringer of the news since he had been the middle man all along.

"It's you again!" Kalulu greeted Nkhoma.

"I bring good news."

"What good news?"

"We have water at last!"

"Do we?"

"Not you! Us! This is where I bring you bad news. You and your family will not be allowed to drink from the well."

"Why not? We have every right to it."

"No, you don't. You didn't dig."

"What's to stop us from using the well?"

26

"There's a guard on it, day and night."

"A guard?"

"Yes! With orders to arrest you if you ever get near the well."

"I see. Who is it?"

"Gwape!"

"Gwape! That stupid self-opinionated conceited little devil?"

"He has his orders."

"We shall see."

And so ended the conversation. Nkhoma went back home satisfied that he had put the fear of death into the hare.

Kalulu was left in a thoughtful mood. His mind was whirling with ideas and plans. The ideas came and went. Some were discarded, others were possibilities worth exploring or modifying. By bedtime, he still had not come up with anything concrete and yet the thirst was unbearable. Kalulu had a very fitful night.

CHAPTER FOUR

Gwape on Guard

To avoid long queues, crowding, and quarrels around the well, the animals took turns to use it. Njobvu used the same schedule he had drawn up for digging the well. So, at the crack of dawn came the antelopes, followed by the bucks, the cheetahs, the deer, and the elephants, all the way down to the warthogs and the zebras. There was no problem in agreeing to this timetable, although the hares were not mentioned, and those at the bottom had to wait for a long time before their turn came.

But cleanliness, decency, and respect for other animals became a major problem. Some animals left the well spotlessly clean. Others wallowed in the well and left the water muddy. There was no problem with the cats: the lion, the leopard, or the cheetah. These were clean animals. It was the snorters and the grunters who spoiled the day for the rest of the animals to follow. Njati, the buffalo, loved to go right into the depths, Mvuu, the hippo, could not resist going under for a complete bath. Then there was Kaphulika, the warthog, and Nguluwe, the wild pig. These never left the well till it was swirling with mud.

In spite of these problems, the schedule was respected by everyone. There were no quarrels between the groups, since most animals drank and left for home in terror of Njobvu's penalties for overstaying and overuse. The fines were heavy. No one dared violate the orders. The heaviest penalty was a complete ban on the whole group using the well for several days. In this way, everyone was a policeman for his own group. He prodded them to get a move on.

Things would have been easier if only individuals were punished. But this collective responsibility was hard to infringe.

Take the case of the hares. No hare was allowed to use the well. Full stop! Kalulu had tried to make a case out of it.

"I and my fellow hares," Kalulu had argued in Njobvu's court, "strongly believe that we are being discriminated against on no grounds at all. Before the well was dug, everyone thought we were intelligent enough to suggest it in the first place. Later, when the water was found, everyone wants to shoot the hares on sight. Yet the well was our creation. It was our baby. We have every right to it."

"You don't have any rights over the well," Njobvu had corrected Kalulu. "You did not help dig it."

"How could we when we were sick/"

"How come you were sick while we were digging and you only got well after the water was found?"

"How could we have known how long the epidemic was going to stay among the hares? One day it was there, the next day it was gone."

"Our ruling, endorsed by all the animals, is that no one who failed to raise a paw or a hoof or a claw to dig the well shall be allowed to use it."

"It's not fair. We will contest it!"

"How will you contest it when all the animals endorsed it?"

"We'll see!"

Gwape went over the court case again in his mind as he sat on his haunches under a *mombo* tree. Kalulu seemed convinced there was a vendetta against him and his kind. Yet the wretched hare could not see the logic of the whole thing. Strangely enough, nothing had been heard of Kalulu since then. It was now almost a week with no sight or sound of him and his family. Gwape wondered how they could survive without water for so long.

29

It was late afternoon. All the animals had come, had drunk their fill for the day, and had gone. Mbizi, the zebra, and his family were the last ones. They would by now be having their naps deep in Nyakalambo forest, till the time came for the next forage. Thinking of naps made Gwape feel like snoozing, too. He leaned against the tree more comfortably and caught himself dropping off several times. He shook himself, got up, and strolled to the edge of the well.

"*Odi!*"

Gwape was startled. He had not heard anyone walk up. Neither was anyone scheduled to come after the zebras. Not until the following day anyway.

"*Odi!*"

Again, the same peremptory voice, behind the *mombo* tree Gwape had been resting under a few minutes before.

"*Odini!*"

Gwape walked uncertainly in the direction of the voice.

"It's me."

"Who's me?"

"Kalulu."

"No! Not you! Go away from this place."

"I've brought you something."

"I said go away. You know this place is restricted for you."

"You'll love the present I brought you."

"What is it?"

"This."

A gourd emerged from the end of a paw behind the tree.

"I don't want it!"

"You don't know what it is."

"Whatever it is, I will have none of it."

30

Kalulu emerged fully and advanced toward Gwape. He dipped a paw into the gourd.

"It's known as *dzakudya-akulu-atamanga*, what's-eaten-when-you're-tied-up." Kalulu's paw came up and smacked some of the substance on Gwape's open mouth. Instinctively, Gwape licked his mouth.

"It's good!"

"You want some more?"

"Yes, please!"

"You can have the whole gourd if you want, but I'll have to tie you up first, according to its name."

"Go ahead. That stuff is sweet."

"I knew you'd love it," Kalulu agreed. "Now sit down here while I tie you up."

Out of nowhere several hares emerged and helped to tie Gwape up.

"Hey! What are you up to? Where did all these hares come from? Stop this nonsense!"

No one stopped the nonsense. After Gwape was truly trussed up, more hares emerged with buckets and proceeded to the well. Gwape's eyes bulged as he squirmed in the ropes. The hares made several trips to the well, while Gwape looked on helplessly. He could not shout, scream or yell. They had also gagged him. The hares left him as he was, under the *mombo* tree. Gwape knew no one would appear till the following morning. It was the thought of what the animals would do to him when they came that ate into his thoughts.

*   *   *

It was the antelopes, the first users in the morning, who raised the alarm.

"Gwape!" They came up to him. "How did you come to be tied up like this?"

"It was Kalulu. He was here!"

"What did he do to you?"

"You can see what he did to me! His mates came, drank, and carried away bucketfuls of water afterward."

"How could you let them do that to you?"

"I didn't. They tied me up first!"

"But how come you allowed yourself to be tied up in the first place?"

"He – Kalulu tricked me!"

"You mean you let him trick you?"

"What difference does it make?"

"It means that all of us, Gwape, will be punished for your stupidity. Wait until Njobvu hears of this."

"I am ruined!"

"You certainly are."

"Aren't you going to untie me?"

"Untie you? So you can make good your escape? No, Njobvu must find you the way we found you."

"I've got cramps all over."

"You will have more when the other animals are through with you. How can you let the cunning little devil enjoy the fruits of our labor when all of us sweated for it days on end?"

"I tell you, it was a trick!"

"You shouldn't have let him within a mile of this place. Those were the instructions."

"He was already here when he did this to me."

"So you were sleeping. You didn't hear him step on the dry leaves and grass. How come you let him touch you?"

"This is not your court. I will wait for Njobvu to interrogate me."

"Oh, quite brave now, aren't you?"

"You can't threaten me."

"Yes, we can. We also sweated to dig that well."

"Just get Njobvu here and I'll explain to him what happened."

One of the sons was sent to raise the alarm and to tell the elephant the bad news. The other antelopes, after drinking, took Gwape to the big baobab tree.

*   *   *

"Tell us," Njobvu began as soon as all the animals had congregated and settled down. "how you came to be tied up like this when your duty was to walk up and down, guarding the well?"

"I have already explained a hundred times," pleaded Gwape. "It was late afternoon. All the animals had drunk and gone. No one was coming until the morrow. In fact, I had got up and walked to the edge of the well when Kalulu crept up behind a tree …."

"But you said the whole tribe attacked you!"

"That was afterward. Let me tell the story my way."

"Proceed. I want the whole court, and all the animals to hear your version and to judge for themselves the truth of the matter and what to do with you afterward."

"Kalulu had this gourd," Gwape began again, trembling at the threat in Njobvu's words.

"A gourd!"

"Yes. It had some delicious things in it."

"How did you know?"

"He smeared the stuff on my mouth."

"He came that close? After the strict orders we gave you, he came to you and held you by your hand and smeared things on your lips?"

"Kalulu is a very persuasive character."

33

"You'll pay for being a persuadable animal. Proceed. What was this stuff in the gourd?"

"*Dzakudya-akulu-atamanga*. That's what it's called."

"And you let yourself be tied up to eat it?"

"It wasn't like that."

"But you were found tied up and there's some sticky stuff around your muzzle."

"It was while he was talking to me that I was overpowered."

"But Gwape, you're bigger than Kalulu."

"I said the whole gang came upon me from behind and manhandled me."

"What happened afterward?"

"They brought buckets and drew some water and took it home with them."

"You realize the hares now have water to last them several days?"

"I do, chief."

Njobvu was very grave. He looked around at the other animals. They too were somber. He looked down at the trussed-up form of Gwape in front of him. Gwape squirmed under the ropes in terror.

"It's all very clear to us," Njobvu pronounced. "You and Kalulu had an understanding whereby you let him draw water in exchange for something. It is also very clear to us what course of action to take: a violation of this kind is punishable by a collective penalty on you and your kind. It is up to the court now to decide on how long you shall be barred from using the well."

CHAPTER FIVE

Fisi on Guard

Fisi, the hyena, was feeling very hungry. Much as he enjoyed the freedom of drinking from the well and taking dips in the water, it did not kill the hunger that he felt all the time. He could not leave the well to forage in the forest. The food which had started growing beside the well was for grazers, not carnivores like him. He could not imagine a worse punishment than to be given the leftovers of his family's meals at home.

"You call this food?" he kept complaining to his wife when she came in the mornings.

"It's all we have left in these difficult times."

"Does your mother call this food?" he would complain to his daughter at midday.

"Do you want me to starve here?" he would protest to his son in the evenings.

As the days went by, he became gloomier and more morose and pugnacious.

"*Odi!*" came a voice from behind the tree, some days later.

"I know that voice," Hyena growled.

"Then why didn't you answer me?" Kalulu emerged from behind the *mombo* tree.

"How dare you come here?"

"I brought you food!"

"You what – what?"

"Look!" Kalulu displayed his wares. "Roast chicken. All nicely done for you!"

"Come here!" Hyena growled again.

"No!" Kalulu scampered away. "You come here!"

"You can't come here waving roast chicken and hope to get away with it."

"You've got to get it first."

Fisi advanced. Kalulu retreated.

"Wait until I catch you."

"You can't catch me."

It went on and on, until Kalulu had drawn Fisi deep into the bush.

"You can have one of these," Kalulu relented.

"Just one?"

"Well, you have been a good friend of mine for some time now. You can have this piece, too."

"Just two?"

"I have some more behind that shrub. We can go and collect it."

"Where did you get it from?"

"I'm now in the chicken business. I sell them live, dead, roast, baked, boiled, broiled, basted, braised. You name it, Kalulu, does it. How would you like them next time?"

"Raw." Hyena licked his lips. "I like them with the blood dripping off them."

"No problem. Tomorrow I'll bring a few. Do you want them whole with the feathers on, or shall we pluck them for you?"

"Whole, please, they taste better when you crunch them with their feathers on."

"You've got yourself a deal."

"Why don't you bring them this evening?"

"I've got to place an order for a large consignment first. Tomorrow same time?"

"Make it earlier."

"I'll try. Bye, then."

"Bye."

Fisi licked his lips, fingers, and all, as he sauntered back to the well. That was the most delicious meal he ever had. At no cost at all.

Wait a minute! At no cost? Why was it free? Fisi was suddenly suspicious. How could Kalulu, the meanest, most cunning little devil, give away roast or raw chicken like that to all and sundry? Well, not all and sundry, just him: Fisi. Kalulu had said they had been friends for so long. What's a chicken or two between friends? Fisi sat under the *mombo* tree and dozed off. He dreamt of raw and bloody chicken drinking from the well.

*   *   *

"Chief Njobvu," Nkhoma went to tell the elephant one mid-morning, "Kalulu and his family don't lack for water these days."

"What do you mean, little one?"

"I met Mrs Kalulu and her daughters yesterday. They were all carrying buckets on their heads. When I asked them, what was in the buckets they said it was earth. What was it for? I asked. They said they were building extensions to their bedroom. I said, 'From the way you are balancing the buckets it couldn't be earth or sand.' They just giggled and went off."

"So what do you think they were carrying?"

"Water."

"Water!"

"Yes, and I think they got it from the well."

"But Fisi is there. He hasn't reported anything to me."

"You know how dopey Fisi is."

"Even if he is stupid he knows what to do when Kalulu comes to the well, let alone the whole family."

"Why don't we go and find out from him?"

"All right, but it had better be a good story. I'm too busy to just go gallivanting around."

"We'll soon know."

"Fisi," Njobvu asked the hyena as soon as they got to the well, "tell us what happened yesterday."

"Nothing happened."

"Didn't Kalulu come here to draw water?"

"Kalulu? No, not him."

"Didn't he come here at all?"

"He came but not to draw water."

"Didn't his wife and daughters come with buckets and draw water from the well?"

"That's not true." Fisi stamped his furiously. "Who told you all these lies? I was here all the time and I would have seen them with my own eyes if they had come with buckets and taken any water."

"All right, then," Njobvu tried again, "What did Kalulu do when he came here?"

"He just came."

"That's all?"

"He said we were old friends and he pitied my long and lonely vigil here at the well."

"And then?"

"He brought me roast chicken."

"And what did you do?"

"I ate it, of course. I was hungry."

"Where did you eat it?"

"Here, I mean there."

"In the bush."

"How far away?"

"Behind those shrubs."

"How many chickens?"

"I didn't count. Maybe three, maybe six."

"So it took you a while to finish them?"

"We were also chatting about old times, the drought, and everything."

"Couldn't his wife and daughters have drawn the water while you were eating those chickens and chatting?"

"I would have heard them."

"But the shrubs over there are a bit far. The well was also hidden from your sight."

"We wanted a quiet shady place."

"With your sworn enemy?"

"But he's not my enemy."

"So he's now your friend?"

"I didn't say that. Kalulu said it."

"Chief Njobvu," interrupted Nkhoma. "Let's go to the well. I bet we will find the hares' tracks all over the place."

"But the other animals have been there already, too."

"Not everywhere. Hares' tracks are very distinctive; even if we can't tell them from the rest at the well itself, we shall know which direction they came from and took afterward."

Sure enough, among the hoofs, paws, and claws were the three distinctive trademarks of the hare. And, as if to confirm Nkhoma's prophecy, the tracks all led in one direction: to the hares' compound.

"You see?" Njobvu growled.

"That was done in Gwape's time," Fisi protested.

"These are fresh tracks. See these droppings by the tree? This is yesterday's work. The hares seem to have had a field day of it, too, and all you could think of was roast chicken."

"Give me another chance, chief," Fisi pleaded. "They did it without my knowledge and consent."

"Your orders were not to admit Kalulu to the well."

"Kalulu did not go to the well at all." Fisi pointed out. "He was with me all the time."

"He has a point," Nkhoma said. "Kalulu himself did not draw the water with Fisi's knowledge. Fisi's duty was to keep him away from the well, which he succeeded in doing."

"Yes, but the rest of the hares succeeded in drawing the water," Njobvu corrected, pondering before he continued. "All right, I will give you another chance. If you let Kalulu or his family draw water again it will be time to change guards."

"Thank you, Chief." Fisi was relieved. "And thank you, Nkhoma."

*   *   *

A week passed, and another. Yet the reports said the hare family had water in plenty. Nkhoma was sent to investigate a second time.

"It's true, Chief," Nkhoma reported back. "The hares don't even need the well. They have their own reservoirs in the back yard."

"Are you sure?"

"Not only that," Nkhoma said vehemently, "They have opened up gardens in the patch behind their compound. They water them every day. I understand they are thinking of growing flowers in the front yard soon, too."

"Even flowers? Such a luxury in a time of drought?"

"I wouldn't put it past the hares. They are up to something all the time."

"But how are they getting the water? Fisi has not reported anything to me."

"Maybe he is afraid to do so."

"Let's go and interrogate him again, more closely this time."

They found a fearful Fisi under the *mombo* tree. They gave him a snack to calm his fears. They chatted about the well and the drought, and then steered the conversation to the hares again.

"We haven't got any feedback from you lately," Njobvu stated. "How are things at the well?"

"They're fine. I would have been the first one to report if they were not."

"You haven't had any visitors?"

"No, none."

"Not even your friend Kalulu?"

"Well, he came but he didn't do anything."

"What did he bring this time?"

"Roast goat."

"Where did you eat it?"

"In the same place."

"But, Fisi, we told you not to move out of sight of the well."

"He wasn't out of my sight."

"No, but his family was."

"What do you mean?"

"The hares have lots of water to spare these days. They have water tanks in the back yard. They have opened up gardens that they are watering every day. Not only that, they are going into the flower business soon. They must be getting the water from somewhere."

"Not from this well."

"Where else?"

"But I didn't let them do it. You have no evidence that they did. All you have are rumors. You can't convict me on hearsay. Who saw the hares drawing water from the well? Tell me and I'll show you a liar."

"He has a point, Chief," Nkhoma said. "If you are going to punish Fisi and his family you need more concrete evidence."

"Isn't the garden concrete enough?"

"It could be growing species able to survive the drought."

"What about the reservoirs?"

"The water could be from anywhere the hares chose to tell us. We couldn't prove them liars without checking the sources, and if I know the hares, the sources could be anywhere between Mtalika and the horizon."

"We need to confer more on this," Njobvu was very pensive. "Come, little one, let's leave Fisi to his duties."

Njobvu and Nkhoma left Fisi by the *mombo* tree. They were still in deep discussion as they walked home.

CHAPTER SIX

The Zombie

Fisi was worried. Two weeks had gone by with nothing happening. But that was not what really worried him. What worried him most was that, if something was going to happen, he could not guess from which direction it would come. And if something happened he would definitely be punished for it. Not only he, Fisi, but all the hyena kind. His wife, children, and relatives would not forgive him for it. Look at what had happened to Gwape and the whole antelope family.

Fisi was worried. He knew that Kalulu would be back with yet another ruse to draw water from the well. He knew Kalulu was aware of his greatest weakness: he could not resist meat of any kind. At the sight of meat, he just lost control of his faculties, obsessed with the desire to get it. He had to get his teeth into the juicy, crunchy portions. He would do anything to get at it.

Fisi was worried. Njobvu and Nkhoma had discovered what he had already suspected, that Kalulu's visits were two-pronged: while Kalulu, the visitor, drew Fisi's attention away, Kalulu's cohorts drew water from the well. While Fisi enjoyed the tasty bits of chicken or goat, gallons and gallons of water were being ferried to the hare village. Fisi could not abandon his meaty meal to chase the hares away. Now everyone knew he was accepting bribes to let the hares get the water they needed. It was true, however, that he had eaten the goat's meat right at the well.

Fisi had refused to be lured away from the well on the pain of fearful punishment. So Kalulu was forced to give Fisi some of the goat, as he went away disappointed. In any case, it was not true that the hares had lots of water, because Kalulu's visit meant that they were running short of it. It could not be true either that the hares had opened up a garden. They could not have drawn so much water that they had a surplus. Fisi had only gone away from the well for a short time and only a short distance away. A bucket or two, maybe, for domestic purposes, but not for irrigating whole gardens. No, Njobvu and Nkhoma were just exaggerating.

Fisi was startled out of his reminiscences by a commotion behind the *mombo* tree. He sat up suddenly, disbelief jumping out of his bulging eyes and open mouth.

"*Kanyama kosenda-senda! Kanyama kosenda-senda!*" came from an animal dripping blood from his body, foaming at the mouth, waving wide ears up and down. The apparition sprang at him, screaming its awful message.

"Help!" Fisi bolted.

"*Kanyama kosenda-senda! Kanyama kosenda-senda!*" The animal chased after him.

"Someone help me," Fisi bawled, as he fled out of sight.

Fisi ran fearfully, as fast as he could, deep into the forest. When he thought he had run deep enough, he stopped, turned, and looked back the way he had come. He breathed hard, his nostrils flared, and his lips quivered. He turned this way and that. Nothing was in sight. The apparition was not on his tail. He listened. No crackling leaves or rustling grass. Where had the thing gone?"

Fisi retraced his steps, looking right and left, and around him all the time. Nothing stirred in the bushes or up the trees. Yet the thing had looked as if it could climb trees or fly. It looked capable of doing anything. Now it had disappeared.

He came back to the well, still fearful, expecting another visitation, but all was quiet. Fisi peeked round the *mombo* tree.

Nothing. He went over to the edge of the well. Nothing was disturbed. He went back to the *mombo* tree and resumed his guard.

Njobvu and Nkhoma found him late in the afternoon.

"Reports have reached us," Njobvu came to the point immediately, "that a fresh supply of water has reached the hares today."

"A thing came this way," Fisi stammered.

"What thing?"

"It looked like a zombie." Fisi shivered as he remembered the incident. "It was uttering frightening things."

"A zombie? How big?"

"Like Nkhoma here."

"Or like Kalulu?"

"Well yes, like Kalulu, too."

"With big ears?"

"Yes, and a bloody body. There was blood all over the place. It's dried up now. I couldn't stand it. I ran away. I was frightened. That's the only time I left the place."

"Where did you go?"

"I just ran as fast as I could. I don't know where I went. My one thought was to get away from the zombie. Zombies are witches and I don't want to die."

"How far did you go?"

"I don't know. I ran and ran, but it couldn't have been very far. I got back as soon as I realized it wasn't following me. I checked, nothing was taken from the well. Everything was all right."

"That was Kalulu. Up to his tricks again."

"It couldn't have been him," Fisi countered.

"He took off his skin."

"He – he what?"

"He removed his skin to scare you off. And it seems he succeeded."

"But I'd recognize Kalulu anywhere. He's my friend. How could he remove his skin like that?"

"He can when he wants to."

"But he was so scary."

"We've had enough of your stories," Njobvu said angrily. "First it was roast chicken, then goat, now it is zombies. And all the time, the hare is stealing our water."

"But I was chased by witchcraft. You would have been scared too, if you saw it."

"Listen Fisi," Njobvu advised. "This is what you are going to do, the next time the zombie comes. Listen carefully, and don't bungle the job this time, or I'll have you and all your kind skinned alive, like the zombie."

"I'm listening."

Njobvu gave Fisi the plan.

"We'll catch him this time!" Fisi was ecstatic. He hopped from one foot to the other. Njobvu and Nkhoma left him alone.

*   *   *

Njobvu's security guards hid at strategic points in the bushes around the well. Nothing happened for several days. A week passed, then another. One afternoon, the guard at the south-eastern side of the well heard the crackling of tiny feet on dry leaves. It was Kalulu. He signaled to the nearest guard, who signaled to the next one. Soon all the guards were alerted, all except Fisi at the well itself.

The guard who had spotted Kalulu observed him closely. He stopped behind a bush and divested himself of his skin. Slowly his skin peeled off from his shoulders, then his arms, his back, and his stomach. Kalulu pulled the skin down over his hips and rolled it away

46

from his thighs, legs, and feet. He stretched it and hung it on a low branch in the shade. He started running toward the well.

"*Kanyama kosenda-senda! Kanyama kosenda-senda!*" he yelled as he ran toward Fisi.

Fisi sat up with a scream.

"Help!" Fisi jumped to his feet and ran off into the bushes.

"*Kanyama kosenda-senda! Kanyama kosenda-senda!*" Kalulu ran after Fisi into the bushes.

Kalulu gave up the chase after a few hundred yards. He turned back to the bush where he had left his skin. It was still where he had left it. He lifted it off the branch and sat down to put it on again. He only got as far as his thighs when he let out a horrendous yell. He pulled it off again and started scratching himself furiously.

"Yah! Aah! *Chitedze!*" he yelled. "Someone put itching beans onto my skin!"

He threw the skin away, rolled on the ground.

"Help!" he roared frothily.

The security guards found him still rolling and scratching on the ground. They pounced on him.

"We've got you!" yelled one of them.

They tied him up and marched triumphantly with him to Njobvu.

"So, my little trickster," Njobvu said gleefully, "you have been caught, at last."

"Give me back my skin!"

"You didn't want it," the guards laughed. "You, yourself, threw it away."

"That's criminal!" Kalulu shouted wrathfully, "To treat someone's skin with *chitedze!*"

47

"You're the criminal," Njobvu corrected him. "You have subjected us to the worst kinds of crime since we dug the well. We will see that you are brought to justice. Your trial is at dawn."

They locked Kalulu in a small hut for the night.

*   *   *

As the night wore on Kalulu grew more and more apprehensive in the small hut. The other animals would surely be merciless. They would choose the most horrible punishment for him, too. They would not bar the hares from using the well, because they had already done that and failed. They had every reason to torture him, and even kill him in the end. As for torture, he had already had a taste of that with the itching beans. Now, here he was, skinless. It would not take long before the skin dried and shrank. Then he would not be able to get back into to. He might even shrink and dry up himself, in the meantime. What a terrible end.

Kalulu blamed himself for being thrown into prison. He had been overconfident. And now they had captured him all too easily. He should not have used the same trick twice. It might have worked on Fisi two or three times, but not on the other animals. Now here he was waiting for his fate, come dawn.

"Kalulu!"

Someone whispered his name outside the door. Kalulu's heart beat wildly against his ribs. It was not dawn yet and, in any case, his captors would not come so stealthily, whispering his name.

"Kalulu!"

"Who is it?" He drew near the door.

"It's me. Fisi!"

"My dear old friend!" Kalulu nearly died of relief.

"What are they going to do to you?"

48

"Do to me?" Kalulu thought fast. "They want to make me the new chief."

"Make you chief?"

"Yes!" Kalulu was still thinking furiously. "They said that after all the cleverness I had shown in getting the water I should be given the title. I had out-tricked all the animal kingdom. They want to make me the king of all tricksters."

"You must be out of your mind."

"Why not? The animals need someone like me to keep them on their toes. They are even now preparing the grandfather of all feasts from dawn to sunset for the crowning."

"That's a lie."

Fisi had not kept abreast of the recent developments. After running away from the well, he had taken some time to return. When he came back, he found all the guards gone. He went home to be told by his wife that they were keeping Kalulu in custody. Fisi had come to find out for himself, but he did not want to announce his presence to all. He comforted himself, however, by saying that he had done everything they had told him to do. Now Kalulu was in their hands. But why should they make him chief instead of punishing him? And what was this about a marathon banquet?

"I don't want to be chief," Kalulu continued. "I told them I did not want to be chief, at all."

"Why not?"

"I can't stand all the pomp and ceremony. Just imagine all the huge feasts I would have to go through everywhere I went. I lead a very uncomplicated life. My diet is very simple for my size, too. I want it to remain that way."

"What are they preparing for you tomorrow?"

"The usual," Kalulu said carelessly. "Chicken, goat, and pig, you know. The choice parts reserved for the new chief, of course."

Fisi's mouth had already started watering, rivulets dripping to the ground.

"How would you like to be the next chief?" Kalulu asked.

"What do you mean?"

"When I told them I didn't want to be chief, they said there was no one else as good as me, but I was free to appoint anyone I wanted to take my place."

"Are you sure?"

"Would I be joking in such a serious matter?"

"What should I do to take your place?"

"If they find you here instead of me, they'll know I have selected you to be the new chief in my place."

"No joking?"

"Just open the door. Njobvu assured me that my word was law until I abdicated."

"But why are you doing this to me?"

"You have been a good friend all along. My family had all the water they needed just because of you. This is my way of thanking you."

Fisi lifted the latch that could only be opened from the outside. Kalulu stepped out.

"Now go in," Kalulu told the hyena. "Tomorrow, when they open the door, just tell them you are the new trickster chief. I crowned you. They will lead you to the grand banquet in great honor. Sleep well, my dear friend."

Fisi went in. Kalulu shut and latched the door. He fled into the nearest bush.

CHAPTER SEVEN

Kamba on Guard

Njobvu, Nkhoma, and other animals had come at dawn and were waiting outside the little prison but. The security guards went and unlatched the door. There was excitement in the morning air. Suddenly there was a commotion inside.

"*Houwiii! Houwiii!*"

"That's not Kalulu!" Nkhoma ejaculated. "That's Fisi!"

"Fisi?" trumpeted Njobvu. "How did he get in?"

"The question is," Nkhoma corrected, "where is Kalulu?"

The security guards emerged with Fisi between them.

"What are you doing here?" roared Njobvu.

"I am your new trickster chief," Fisi announced.

"What?"

"Kalulu didn't want to be chief. So he let me take his place."

"Are you out of your mind?" Njobvu looked as if he would explode any minute. "Guards, tie up that crazy animal."

"This is no way to treat a chief," Fisi howled.

"Who told you that you were a chief?"

"I told you, I exchanged places with Kalulu," Fisi protested. "You should keep your promises. I demand justice."

"Where is Kalulu?"

"He left last night."

"How did he leave? Who let him out? How did you get here?"

"One question at a time. I can't answer them all at once."

"You have to!" Njobvu was beside himself. "Guards! Put him back inside. Find out from him, whichever way, what happened."

"We're in trouble now," Nkhoma remarked.

51

"What do you mean 'we'?" Njobvu turned to Nkhoma. "HE is in trouble."

"Kalulu is at large again," Nkhoma explained. "And you know what that means."

"You're right; we're back to where we started." Njobvu shook his head desperately. "We need to place another guard at the well at once."

He turned to the other animals. They shrank back as he looked them over. No one wanted to be the next victim.

"Who is going to guard the well?"

"Not me!" said Mkango.

"Not me!" snorted Mvuu.

"I don't fancy that job," said Mbizi. A lot of the other animals refused to take up the post.

"No one is going to volunteer," Nkhoma observed. "You'll have to appoint someone. It is your job as chief to do that."

"I will go!" Kamba, the tortoise, crawled forward from between the buffalo's feet.

"You!" Njobvu was incredulous as he looked at the tiny shell crawling on unsteady legs toward him.

"I can try," Kamba said timidly. "I mean I'll try to succeed."

"Let him try," Nkhoma advised. "After all Gwape and Fisi also tried."

"All right, we'll let him try, although, looking at him, you'd think we might as well invite all the hares to a water-drinking and swimming gala."

"Give him a chance."

"Brothers and sisters," Njobvu started a speech, "you have all seen and heard for yourselves. Our prisoner has escaped. And we now expect our adversary to attack at any time. This time there will be no half measures: we kill on sight!"

"Kill on sight!" The chant was taken up by all the animals. "K.O.S. Kill On Sight. K.O.S."

"Kill On Sight" became the code words for "Operation Kalulu."

*   *   *

It was late afternoon. All the animals had drunk their fill and had retired. Kalulu, now in his full skin again, emerged from the bush and walked stealthily toward the *mombo* tree. He peeped behind the *mombo* tree. There was no one in sight. He stepped into the open, walked a tentative step or two, looked left and right. No one challenged him.

"*Odi!*"

Silence.

"*Odi!*"

Silence.

"I have brought *dzakudya-akulu-atamanga*."

No answer.

That's odd, Kalulu thought. That's disappointing, I should say. No one guarding the well? No one expecting me?

"I said, I have bought *dzakudya-akulu-atamanga*," he shouted to the empty air.

Still no response.

Kalulu advanced toward the well. It was where it was before. The rope, the bucket, the pulley were still in place. There were some rocks and tree stumps around the edge for the animals to step on if they did not want to touch the mud or the puddles around the edge of the well. Everything was quiet.

Kalulu looked right and left again. Maybe they did not expect him to come back so soon. That was why there was no guard at the well.

"Hmm!" He cleared his throat.

No challenge.

Kalulu went boldly up over the rocks and stumps. He stood at the edge of the well and looked down the shaft. He got giddy and shut his eyes to steady himself. He released the bucket and lowered it down. After a minute, there was a splash as the bucket hit the water below. He tugged at it and started pulling it back up. So there was no problem getting the water this time. No bribery, no zombies, nothing.

The bucket came up to the top and Kalulu reached for it. He lifted it up to the edge of the well. He stepped on another rock to do so. He hefted the bucket onto the edge of the hole. Now was the time to call the rest of the gang. He turned and stepped back to tell them that all was clear. He lifted a leg and suddenly found he could not move it. He tugged but could not lift it off the rock. He tried another leg but it too had got stuck fast.

"Rock," Kalulu begged, "let me go!"

No answer.

He tried the third leg. No motion. It was stuck, too, as was the fourth.

"Rock! Let me go!" he shouted.

No response.

"This is a trick!" he screamed. "You got me stuck here so the animals can get at me."

"Yes!" came the answer. "I've got you at last!"

"Who are you?"

"Kamba!"

"Kamba!" Kalulu was amazed. "What did I do to you? Release me this instant!"

"I can't!"

"If you let me go I will let you have all the *dzakudya-akulu-atamanga*."

"I said I can't. You're standing on my shell."

"How did you do that?"

"Just a little bit of glue, that's all. You thought I was a stump or a rock, didn't you? You clever-by-half tricksters annoy me; that's why I volunteered to catch you. Just look at you, now. How pathetic you look, all stuck up like a trussed chicken! Wait until the other animals come."

"Please!" Kalulu whimpered. "I'll give you anything you ask."

"You know about the K.O.S. don't you!"

"K.O.S.?" Kalulu asked hoarsely. "What is K.O.S.?"

"Kill On Sight."

"Kill who on sight?"

"Kill Kalulu, of course! Wait until I signal for the rest to come."

Kamba whistled, a loud penetrating whistle. Kalulu trembled violently as he heard the crackling of a lot of hooves and paws on leaves and grass. Njobvu and Nkhoma came to the clearing, flanked by the rest of the animals. Kalulu released his bowels.

"Forgive me," he managed to say.

"My cunning little friend," Njobvu was jubilant, "This time you won't escape."

"I will not do it again."

"You are beyond forgiveness, my friend."

"I will dig another well for you all. My brothers and sisters will dig several wells."

"You should have helped dig this one. Everything would have been all right."

"I had – we had diarrhea!"

"You have diarrhea right now!"

55

All the animals laughed gleefully, pointing at his soiled hindquarters.

"We are wasting time," Kamba protested from under his burden. "Get him off my back, will you?"

"Wait!" Kalulu yelped. "I will reveal to you how to kill me."

"What do you mean?"

"Hares don't get killed that easily. You remember you took my skin? Well, I didn't die, did I? I've got a new skin now. How did I do that? That's a secret. And there's also another secret of how to kill a hare."

"How do you die?"

"Smash my head against *dzira-la-ndikunyenga*."

"*Dzira-la-ndikunyenga?*"

"Yes, it is a rare bird but it is lethal to hares."

"Where can I find it?"

"It's in my gourd. If you place it on that tuft of grass there, grab me by the tail, and thump! You'll see me dead within seconds."

Njobvu grabbed Kalulu by the back legs as Nkhoma placed a small egg they had discovered in the hare's gourd on a tuft of grass. The other animals followed all the activities with great interest. They crowded round the elephant, the cliff-hopper and the hare.

"Kill on sight!" they chanted. "Kill Kalulu on sight!"

"Tell my wife and children," Kalulu prayed, "that I'm dying for them today."

"You are indeed dying today," Njobvu said. He shifted his grip from the legs to the tail. The tail, however, was so short he could not get a good grip. As he swung the body up to fling it on the egg, Kalulu slipped off, bounced on the tuft of grass and fled between Njobvu's legs.

"Kalulu! Kalulu!" the animals roared as they shuffled and tried to stamp on the hare, as he dodged past them. But Kalulu gave them the slip. He disappeared behind the *mombo* tree.

"He's escaped!" Njobvu groaned as he sat down wearily.

"Yes, again!" Nkhoma reminded him.

Njobvu could not lift his eyes to meet those of his fellow animals. He could not bear to see their accusing eyes.

"But," Njobvu brightened up a bit. "There's some comfort yet."

"What comfort?" Nkhoma asked.

"We will kill Fisi in his place."

"Oh, that fellow, I had forgotten about him."

"Let's go and get him!" Njobvu led the way.

"Kill on sight!" shouted the animals. "Kill Hyena on sight!"

The animals trooped after their chief back to the village.

"It looks as if it is going to rain."

"What?"

Nkhoma was sniffing the air. Njobvu did the same. The animals stopped and followed their example. Yes, there was a sudden dampness in the breeze. They looked up into the sky. Clouds were gathering on the horizons.

"Salvation!" the animals cheered.

"Let's hurry!" Njobvu said. "We don't want the rain to spoil our fun."

The security guards unlatched the door of the hut. They rushed in and brought out the trussed form of Fisi. They dumped him unceremoniously on the ground.

It had now started drizzling.

"You freed Kalulu," Njobvu accused. "He has escaped again. Now you will die in his place."

"That's unfair," Fisi whined. "Look at the sky. Look at the drizzle. The full rains will be with us any moment. You can't punish me now that the rains are back with us."

"You think so?" Njobvu stamped where he stood.

"He has a point, you know," Nkhoma interjected. "We should be bringing out our buckets to collect the deluge. We should be rejoicing for the end of the drought instead of killing this poor unfortunate creature. Now that Kalulu has escaped and the rains are here there will be no need to guard the well. There will be water everywhere. Kalulu will keep on laughing and tricking us as long as we let him do so. It's not Hyena's fault."

"Let him go, Chief," chanted the animals.

"Free the hyena!" chorused everyone.

"Maybe you're right!" Njobvu said at last. "Instead of killing each other we should be singing and dancing. The drought is ended. The rains are here at last!"

THE END

GLOSSARY

(Note: The vernacular names of the animals have been translated in the story itself.)

Chitedze:	Itching beans
Dambo:	Low-lying wet ground
Dzakudya-akulu-atamanga:	As in the story, literally, "what's-eaten-when-you're tied-up."
Dzira-la-ndikunyenga:	Literally, "egg-of-I-am-cheating-you"
Kanyama kosenda-senda:	Literally, "a little skinned animal"
Mombo:	A type of tree
Ndakupha:	Literally, "I have killed you." In the story, it means "I have scored against you"
Nsikwa:	As in the story, a game played with spinning tops
Odi:	A verbal knock at the door
Odini:	The acknowledgement to "Odi!"